Understanding the Prophetic Ministry
A Training Manual for Prophets

Apostle Ruben Martinez, D.Min.

Understanding the Prophetic Ministry

A Training Manual for Prophets

Apostle Ruben Martinez, D.Min.

Copyright © 2020 by Ruben Martinez

ISBN: 978-1-61529-229-5

Vision Publishing
P.O. Box 1680
Ramona, CA 92065
1 760 789-4700
www.booksbyvision.org

All rights reserved worldwide.

No part of this book may be reproduced in any manner without the written permission of the author except in brief quotations embodied in critical articles of review.

Tabke of Contents

Author Foreword 5

Foreword 7

Acknowledgements 9

Chapter One: Understanding the Prophetic Ministry 13

Chapter Two: The Growing Pains of the Prophet and the Ministry 17

Chapter Three: Understanding the Power of the Prophet 21

Chapter Four: Prophets Will Contest Sin 25

Chapter Five: Only a Prophet Can Train a Prophet 29

Chapter Six: The Transfer of the Mantle 33

Chapter Seven: Elisha's Request for the Double Portion of the Spirit of Elijah 37

Chapter Eight: What Are the Characteristics of a True Prophet? 41

Chapter Nine: A Prophet in the Old Testament 51

Chapter Ten: Who Is the Prophet in the Bible? 55

Chapter Eleven: Do You Know the Time? 59

Appendix: Descriptions of the Prophets 63

Author Foreword

This manual is dedicated to God the Father, God the Son Jesus, and God the Holy Spirit. The Lord spoke to me and said that He wanted me to write this manual. It has taken the better part of a year to complete this assignment. It was hard for me to write because I had writers' block. I just did not have the confidence to write. But God spoke to me and said that all I had to do was to sit and He would give me what I would write. I did not start writing immediately. I kept putting it off. He said to me that I could write if I would just sit down with Him. He would teach me what to write. He also told me that I needed to stop getting distracted with other things. For example, I am a big Yankees fan and I also have a Bible school to run. I was working and doing a lot of teaching and I was also coaching a girls' basketball team. I kept running, until December 26, 2019. On that day, I had to chaperone the team with the head coach and some of the parents. It was a weekend trip, but I was determined. I said to myself that I would begin to write the manual that God told me write. On the first night I started writing. I wrote one page the whole weekend. I stopped at that point and then Covid19 came. Along with my other responsibilities, I was also taking care of my 92 year old father. Well, I started to write again in March. Work and basketball had stopped. I had to go to Georgia because I was looking for a house, so my wife and I traveled there in July. My father took ill while I was away that weekend. I had called my father, but he did not answer, so I called my granddaughter to check up on him. I called my brother, as well, so the family went to the house and found him unresponsive. When I got home, the same thing happened two more times. I took him to the hospital and found out that his insulin was killing him. My father had been a diabetic, but at some point, the diabetes went away; my father did not have diabetes anymore. This set me back on my writing, but I wrote some, every time I had a moment. In time, things were going well until my wife fell down six steps and hurt herself badly. My wife had been diagnosed with a small enlargement of her heart, on the right side. I had been praying for her as I always do. She stayed in the hospital for four days. The doctor told us that there was nothing wrong with her heart. We were so blessed! God is still healing and doing miracles. Thus, I want to dedicate this manual to my wife and to my daughters for being so understanding and allowing me the time that I needed to write. I also want to thank Evangelist Euphemia Strauchn for helping with corrections. Finally, I want to thank each of the people that took time to read the manual and give their comments. This has been extremely challenging for me, but I am so grateful that God got me through it.

Apostle Ruben A. Martinez, D.Min.

Foreword

I have had the pleasure of knowing this mighty man of God for approximately 30 years. Apostle Martinez writes under the inspiration of Holy Spirit. He is truly a man after God's own heart. His journey has not been an easy one. He has truly been trained and equipped by Holy Spirit as a Prophet of the Most High God.

Apostle Martinez is living proof to us today that God truly uses ordinary people to do an extraordinary work. His humble beginnings consisted of years of drug addiction, life struggles, pain, and imperfections. Through it all God's hand was upon him. Even in the hardest of times he was aware that God was with him.

I am a witness that the man of God lives what he writes about. Many years ago, as he began to move in his prophetic calling, church leaders attempted to shut him down. He tells us in this powerful book that prayer is always at the front of every assignment. That is where the word of God will come. He reminds us that our help comes from God. He says that the prophet must always trust in God and God alone.

Through much prayer, fasting and meditation I witnessed the man of God walk away from a Church and a Church family he loved to follow the leading of Holy Spirit to a place where he would be trained and equipped to come forth as a Prophet of the Most High God!

As Apostle Martinez shares with us in this dynamic book "The training of a prophet is very rigorous, and the prophet is always in training". He says that when the person is called into the office of the prophet, that is the starting of the training. The training starts with the voice of God, no man can do the calling of the office of the prophet. He warns us that being called does not mean you go out on your own.

Apostle Martinez a seasoned very inspiring, most powerful Prophetic Apostle has had a long history of moving in his prophetic office. Following the leading of Holy Spirit, he has taken the time to clarify the nature of what it truly means to be a Prophet called by God. Holy Spirit has deemed him qualified to teach God's people as one who loves and has the heart of the Father.

I am one of Apostle Martinez's Spiritual Daughters. I have had the pleasure of being trained, equipped, and affirmed into my prophetic office by this awesome man of God. As he tells us in this dynamic book, the prophet is always in training. I am truly a witness that he stands by all that he has written in this manual.

Apostle Martinez has written a powerful training manual for Prophets. From the beginning of this book you will feel and sense his personal journey as a seasoned Prophet called by God. From the beginning of this book we find that to have a call is not enough. It is only the beginning of an amazing journey.

Apostle Martinez covers step by step the call to the office of the Prophet, the obedience, the training, the persecution and more. From the beginning of the book Apostle Martinez takes the time to explain to the reader the nature of the prophetic experience at every level. As a Prophet called by God himself who has truly experienced the highs and lows of this tremendous call he writes from years of experience as well as extensive research.

This powerful book Understanding the Prophetic Ministry, A Training Manual for Prophets is a valuable tool. This book is and will be valuable to us as well as generations to come.

Pastor Prophetess Sandra E. Dukes
Divine Revelation Ministry of Restoration Inc.
Lovejoy, Georgia

Acknowledgements

Thank you, Apostle Martinez, my wife, and I are honored to have you as our Spiritual Father. We have been empowered by your teaching. We are witnesses to the fact that you have the heart of the Father. We thank you for sharing some of your unlimited experiences as a true Prophet of God. Many will be blessed by this book for years to come!

Pastor Prophet Bernard Dukes
Divine Revelation Ministry of Restoration Inc.
Lovejoy, Georgia

A great manual that will train prophets to sound the trumpet to bring forth the awakening of the bride of Christ in this hour. A tool that will activate and sharpen the gift to hear God's voice to deliver His message to His people.

Minister Adina Ben Yehuda
Cornerstone Ministries, Inc.
Staten Island, NY.

Apostle DR. Ruben Martinez, understanding the prophetic ministry of the prophet and prophetic anointing comes through loud and clear. His teaching on the importance of training for the office of the prophet could not have come at a better time. Thank you for this gift that is a reminder of protocol and doing things in decency and order when called by the highest God.

Evangelist Euphemia Strauch
Cornerstone Ministries, Inc.
Staten Island, NY.

A quick and easy read in gaining biblical insight into the office of the Prophet, which oftentimes is a misunderstood ministry. Extensive scriptural references in outlining the office of a prophet, the call, the training, and the preparation prior to the commissioning.

Rev. Tammy C. Stradford, LCPC.
President, Rhema Prayer Ministries
Staten Island, NY.

I was very much encouraged by the reading of Apostle Martinez's book, "The Training Manual for Prophets". I have known Apostle Martinez for well over twenty years and my wife, Mercedes has known him for over fifty years. Apostle Martinez mentions in his book that God appoints the prophets and once you are called by God, you have to train. It is a process you must go through. This is in fact true, as over the years, I have seen Apostle Martinez submit himself to training in ministry under his spiritual father.

Evangelist Billy and Mercedes Williams
D.R.M.R. Ministry

I found this book to be a must read for anyone that aspires to a life in the prophetic Ministry. This book gives insight and addresses the most common problems one encounters in this walk of life. It also gives helpful and achievable solutions to empower everyone to become the person God created he or she to be. I recommend this book for every ministry head.

Deacon Perry Johnson
Seeds of Greatness Bible Church
New Castle, Delaware

Many times in scripture we see how God raised prophets to bring His people closer to Him or to bring correction, or to warn them of impending catastrophe or judgment. In this time of national unrest and confusion, Apostle Ruben Martinez's second book sheds a much-needed light on the office of the prophet, and the " growing pains" encountered by those God calls to this office. This book is an indispensable tool in the arsenal of the man or woman of God who knows that in these uncertain times, more than ever, our communities need prophets who have their ear to the heart of God and who can confidently declare "thus sayeth the Lord".

Rev. Lester Figueroa, Sr. Pastor
Calvary Assembly of God
Staten Island, NY.

The scripture is clear as it relates to being trained for ministry. Twice in chapters two and three of 1 Samuel, it is mentioned of Samuel the budding prophet, that he ministered unto the Lord "before" Eli the priest. The word before means, "in front of". We can translate those verses in the following way, "And the child Samuel ministered unto the Lord in the presence of or under the oversight of Eli the priest". First notice that Samuel was immature, just a child in understanding spiritual things and needed guidance. Secondly, he submitted to the training, leadership, and oversight of his mentor.

Apostle Martinez's manual for prophets, is a great starting place to lay a foundation in the lives of upcoming prophets for this next season in the Kingdom of God. Having the right mentor and the right training will prove to be invaluable to those called to the ministry of the prophet (cf. 1 Sam. 2:11, 3:1).

Apostle Emil Cedeno
Risen Son Ministries
Moreno Valley, CA.

Understanding the Prophetic Ministry by Apostle Ruben Martinez is an excellent read for anyone who desires to operate in the prophetic and who wants to better equip themselves to walk in it. Not only will you learn how to hear His voice, but you will also learn how to identify your prophetic call and flow in the prophetic gifts. This book is a must read if you have a prophetic calling.

Dr. Tony V. Lewis
President & Founder
Christian Bible Institute & Seminary
Houston, TX

Thank you, Apostle Ruben Martinez, for this prophetic ministry manual. This is a good place to start and grow in prophetic ministry. This manual unveiled one of the reasons a pastor cannot effectively train a prophet. This book is thumbs up. Heaven's best and Higher favor!

Supreme Archbishop Emmanuel OjoPowerson

Chapter One:
Understanding the Prophetic Ministry

John 1:1 In the beginning was the word, and the word was with God, and the word was God.

In the beginning God spoke prophetically, when he said let there be light in the first chapter of the book of Genesis.

The word was spoken in the beginning, with a purpose; to take form. When the word is spoken to a person it begins to form and take shape in the person. Just as God began to speak the world into existence, and it took form, when the word is spoken to a person it begins to shape and form that person into the plan and purpose of God. He or she that is called to the ministry of the Prophet must first hear the word of God before he or she can move in or understand the call. Having a call is just the beginning. The next thing that must happen is the hearing of the word that has come. Without the word, the person cannot be formed and shaped.

In Jeremiah 18: 1-4 we are told, *"The word which came to Jeremiah from the Lord, saying, Arise, and go down to the potter's house, and there I will cause thee to hear my words."* So, we see that the word has come to take form and take shape. No word no shape! *"Then I went down to the potter's house, and behold, He wrought a work on the wheels. And the vessel that he made of clay was marred in the hand of the potter: so, he made it again another vessel, as seemed good to the potter to make it."*

The word is now in action, beginning to form and take shape in the person. In time, we get to see the shaping of the person on whom God has placed a call. When God puts His hand on a person, He is looking at a lump of clay that He designed and which he will shape with His hand. He now has reshaped it, so that it will do His will.

To summarize what we have learned:

1. God spoke prophetically in Genesis chapter 1.
2. The word came to Jeremiah.
3. God said I will cause thee to hear my words.

Verse 5 *"Then the word of the Lord came to me, saying,"*

Verse 6 *"O house of Israel, cannot I do with you as this potter? Saith the Lord. Behold, as the clay is in the potters' hand, so are ye in mine hand, O house of Israel."*

Give notice to verse 5 and 6. In verse 5 we are told *"then the word came to me saying,"* 6… *"cannot I do with you as this potter?"* It is God that does the doing, and the saying, by releasing His word to the prophet that He has chosen for the work. Before anyone can go out to do any work for the Kingdom of the Lord he or she must submit themselves to the hands of the potter. We can see that there needs to be training in order to move forward. Being in the hands of the potter is the most important place to hear God from. In order for God to do the work, the prophet must be ready to lay down their will, so the will of God can be done for the work that will come from the potter's hand. Looking at Jeremiah 18 is a must for anyone that is called to the ministry of the prophet when understanding and wisdom are needed. You must have direction before you can go. So, the first instruction is hearing the word of God, to come into His presence, to be formed in the spirit, meaning His spirit; remember that He is the potter.

To summarize what we have learned:

1. God reminds the prophet "Cannot I do with you as this potter".
2. Behold: see the clay, how God shapes the prophet.
3. The prophet is shaped in the potter's hand.

A Larger View

Prophets can speak a word concerning a nation and kingdom. Let us look at verses 7 – 9.

Verse 7 *"At what instant I shall speak concerning a nation, and concerning a kingdom, to pluck up, and to pull down, and to destroy it;"* verse 8 *"If that nation, against whom I have pronounced, turn from their evil, I will repent of the evil that I thought to do unto them."* Verse 9 *"And at what instant I shall speak concerning a nation, and concerning a kingdom, to build and to plant it,"*

In verses 7, 8 and 9 comes instruction for the prophet, which will connect to chapter 1:10. It also gives direction to what God wants the prophet to do. God is teaching the prophet how to speak. Hearing, following instruction and direction will help the person develop his or her ministry.

Let us summarize what we have learned:

1. God speaks concerning a nation and a kingdom through the prophet.
2. Prophets pluck up, pull down and destroy evil in nations and kingdoms against whom God has made a pronouncement.
3. Prophets can build and plant nations and kingdoms

Training is Essential

Prophets should not go forth without being trained. God trains the ear gate of the person in whom He has called to the ministry of the prophet. Jeremiah is given specific instructions for the assignment. He or she that is called to the prophet's ministry must train. Prophets are always in training, learning, and hearing from God. Prophets are trained in the desert where no one can disturb them while in training. The purpose of training is to hear the voice of God, feel His presence, and smell His aroma, learning when to speak and when to be silent, not to release a word before its time. Training is necessary to understand the timing of God. Learning to move with God and not before, Jeremiah did not move or say anything without first hearing from God. God will not use anyone that is not willing to train in the desert. Learning in the desert will teach you how to respond from the desert experience. The desert is where you learn in the spirit the things of the spirit. Learning with God is to learn in the deep and not the shallow ground. The desert teaching takes us high into the spirit realm, as we learn to depend on God to supply all our needs.

Prophets are called to pray and to intercede. The Father wants children that are willing to learn His ways. The desert is the place of training. In this teaching we see God training the prophet how to preach. When a person is called to the ministry of the prophet, he, or she, must remember that they must be in training. All prophets are not the same and do not train the same.

Chapter Two:
The Growing Pains of the Prophet and the Ministry

The growing pains of the prophet begins in the womb of the spirit. Let us look at what God tells Jeremiah in chapter 1:4-5. When God speaks, He speaks in detail and direction for His purpose to be done. Purpose and direction come from the spiritual realm. It will then manifest in the natural. Looking at verse 4, *"Then the word of the Lord came unto me saying,"* verse 5 *"Before I formed thee in the belly I knew thee, and before thou camest forth out of the womb I sanctified thee, and I ordained thee a prophet unto the nations."*

Man does not appoint the prophet. He is appointed by God. We see the word I is used 4 times and the word thee is used 3 times. Take notice that God uses I and thee to get the attention of Jeremiah. I formed you in the belly and I knew you in the belly. This is direct, before you came forth out of the womb. Jeremiah's ear is being trained to hear the voice of God in the spiritual womb, in the realm of the spirit of God. In order to enter the spiritual realm of God you have to be called to enter. Not everyone is called to this realm. God then tells Jeremiah, I sanctified you, I set you apart and declared you Holy and ordained you a Prophet to the nations.

Let us summarize what we have learned:

1. The word of the Lord came to Jeremiah.
2. God formed the prophet Jeremiah in the belly.
3. God knew Jeremiah before he came out of the womb.
4. God sanctified Jeremiah and set him apart.
5. God ordained Jeremiah a prophet to the nations.

In verses 6 - 7 we see the pain that Jeremiah starts to feel. Why is he feeling that way? Is it because he is young and does not feel that he can do what God is telling him to do? He has doubt and he tells God that he cannot speak because he is a child. God then answers him and tells him not to say that he is a child. God then tells Jeremiah, I will send you and you will speak whatsoever I command you to speak. God tells him not to be afraid of their faces, I am with you to deliver you. God puts His hand out and touches Jeremiah's mouth. God tells Jeremiah that He put His words in Jeremiah's mouth, that he has set him over the nations, over the kingdoms, to root out and to pull down, and to destroy, and to throw down, to build, and to plant. The training took place in the womb.

Looking at the word of God, we find that there are only three people that are to be prophets from the womb: Jeremiah, John the Baptist, and Jesus the Christ. These are the only people in the entire bible that get their assignment in the womb. Other prophets are called outside of the womb. These are the prophets that are trained in the desert.

The desert is a lonely place. It is where Moses was trained. God does not send anyone on assignment without being trained for the assignment. The growing pains of the prophet are many. When you say you cannot God says you can, because I have put my word in your mouth. Growing to be a prophet is not easy, and you are always in training, because there is always going to be a new assignment.

Jeremiah is called to the office of the prophet before his birth. The Lord told him to encourage him and to assure him. Jeremiah was about 20 years of age when his call is confirmed and showed reluctance and hesitation in being a prophet. Even today many are called to the office of the prophet and have the same feelings that Jeremiah had. Those called today to the office of the prophet today should pray and ask God to help them.

Anyone that is called to the office of the prophet should become connected with a seasoned prophet and should go to a school for prophets, so that they can get the proper training.

Prayer is particularly important for a novice. If called to the office of the prophet it does not mean that you go out on your own. You cannot be the officer if you do not know anything of the office. Learning is particularly important, the protocol, learning when to speak and when to be silent. Learn to hear the voice of God, learn when to move and when not to move. Learning when to release a word and when to hold the word, and learning how to see in the spiritual realm. Learning when to lay hands on people and when not to. Many think that being a prophet is the ultimate. It is not! To become a prophet, it takes a lot of training. Being called is the beginning of the process.

Let us summarize what we have learned:

1. Do not make excuses as to why you cannot be a prophet.
2. God can send whomever He chooses.
3. Speak only what God commands you to speak.
4. Do not be afraid of their faces.
5. The Lord will put His words in your mouth.

We can see very clearly the intense training that comes with being called to the office of the prophet. There are many who claim to be prophets. But, when you ask them if they have had training, and who have they trained under, they cannot give you an answer. Instead, they may say I do not need help from anyone to train me. God will train me. Yes, God will train you, but He will also send a spiritual father - mother to help train you. I know because I have gone through it! Even at this time in my life I still seek the help that I need. One of the lessons that I have learned is to get help and not be too proud to get it.

Never put yourself in a position where you think you know it all, because when you do, you will fall flat on your face. A novice prophet is vulnerable when he or she tries to do it on their own. The meaning of novice: one that is new, untrained, unskilled, and uninitiated in a call or profession according to the Prophet's Dictionary, By Dr. Paula A. Price.

Jeremiah was raised up to preach judgment is coming. Jeremiah has his assignment and his training. Jeremiah signifies "one raised up by the Lord." The Matthew Henry Commentaries Study Bible tells us sin brings the judgment of God, but if His people will repent, He will forgive, and national judgment may be temporarily postponed. You will find that each prophet has a different assignment, but the one common part of the assignment will always be teaching repentance.

Prophets are the apple of God's eye. Prophetic appointment include: the call and installation of a prophet in the office to serve in its official capacity. This phrase speaks to the prophet's completion of the procedures, training, grooming, and endorsement by mentors and senior prophets as evidence of God's release. The word for such standing is the Hebrew term 'amad'. It speaks to one being appointed to a leadership position with governing authority as used in 1 Samuel 19:20, (taken from the Prophet's Dictionary, Dr. Paula A. Price).

Chapter Three:
Understanding the Power of the Prophet

The power of the prophet comes from the word that God speaks through the prophet. The prophet does not speak on his own accord, he or she speaks at the will of God. The power that comes from the prophet comes from the word that God speaks. Words have power to do and undo. Words have energy and power with the ability to help, to heal, to hinder, to hurt, to harm, to humiliate, and to humble. Considering the powerful force of the words we utter, we must discipline ourselves to speak in a way that conveys respect, gentleness, and humility. Taken from the Huff Post, "We can see that words have power."

When the prophet opens his or her mouth to release the word of God, it is going to come in power. That word is going to make something happen and it will be powerful. When God speaks, His word acts. Isaiah 55:11 says, "So shall my word be that goeth forth out of my mouth: it shall not return unto me void, but it shall accomplish that which I please, and it shall prosper in the thing where I sent it."

Let us summarize what we have learned:

1. Remember to consider the powerful force of the words we utter. Words have power.
2. Words hurt or heal.
3. Words can humiliate.
4. Words can hinder or help.
5. Words can bless or curse.
6. We must discipline ourselves.

Let us look at Isaiah 55:11. *"So shall my word be that goeth forth out of my mouth."* We can see that God is saying "my word" and is releasing the word saying that it is His.

It shall not return unto me void; it is going to do what it is sent to do. It shall accomplish. God will accomplish what He says to the prophet. The prophet speaks what is being spoken to him or her. We must remember that the word belongs to God and shall prosper where He sends it. His word will prosper in a person or a nation, which ever pleases Him! Thus we must understand the power that is generated in the prophet. Having an understanding of the word, you will know it is the word of God that gives the power to the prophet to speak!

Let's take a look at 1 Kings 17 verse 1:

> *"And Elijah the Tishbite, who was of the inhabitants of Gilead, said unto Ahab, As the Lord God of Israel liveth, before whom I stand, there shall not be dew nor rain these years, but according to my word."*

As we can see, according to the word of the prophet that is being spoken, Elijah is releasing the word of God, released by the spirit of God. Elijah is hearing what God is speaking to him in the spirit realm, and that allows him to release it in the natural realm. Elijah is connected in the spirit realm and can hear what is being said. Elijah understands that the power he has comes from hearing God. To release a word, it must have power. That power comes from God. Power is generated from above, then it is sent down. When Peter was in prison, the church prayed, and power came down. Peter was released from prison.

One has to have a strong relationship with God to recognize the power of the word. When we look at Elijah, we see the relationship he had with God and what his prayer life was like. Elijah had the understanding, of the word of God and the power that came with it. Looking at Elijah he appears on the scene suddenly, with the power of the word of God in his mouth. His words were "there shall be no rain". He is fed by ravens at the word of God. God tells him to go to the brook of Cherith. Then he was told to go to Zarephath. God tells him that He has commanded a widow to sustain him. In verse 14,

> *"For thus saith the Lord God of Israel, The barrel of meal shall not waste, neither shall the cruse of oil fail, until the day that the Lord sendeth rain upon the earth."*

Why does he tell her that she would not lose anything? The prophet Elijah heard from God and tells the widow woman to fear not. The prophet instructs the widow woman to make him a cake and bring it to him, then make her and her son a cake to eat. Because of her obedience to the word of the prophet, the Lord God of Israel said that the meal and the oil would last "until the day that the Lord sendeth rain upon the earth." That is powerful. That is the word of the Lord! In verse 15 we learn that she did according to the saying of Elijah: and she, and he, and her house, did eat many days. Verse 16 "And the barrel of meal wasted not, neither did the cruse of oil fail, according to the word of the Lord, which he spake by Elijah." The word that Elijah spoke came to pass and it was fulfilled.

There is a lot that takes place in 1 Kings chapter 17. The widow woman's son dies, Elijah cried unto the Lord and the child is brought back to life. Verse 24 *"And the woman said to Elijah, now by this I know that thou art a man of God, and that the word of the Lord in thy mouth is truth."* Everything that came out of the mouth of the prophet Elijah was truth and came to pass. In 1 Kings chapter 17 we see four miracles take place.

To summarize what we have learned:

1. The woman fed Elijah, she ate, and her son ate.
2. The barrel of meal did not waste, and the oil did not fail.
3. The child was brought back to life.
4. The food and oil would last until the Lord sent rain.

A prophet speaks the mind and the heart of God. God does not lie. He is the way, the truth, and the life. Life is given by the word of God. God knows who has His heart and His mind. Not every word released is the word of God. When a word is given, one should not accept a word without praying to make sure that the word is from God. When someone prophesies and they say, "Do you receive it?" just say I will pray about it. When a word is released it will line up with what God has already spoken to that person. Many times the word of the Lord was given to me, and if it did not match what God had spoken to me, I would not receive it. I would also tell that person that God had not spoken that word. It is especially important to test the word that is being released. The bible tells us in 1 John verse *1 "Beloved, believe not every spirit, but try the spirits whether they are of God: because many false prophets are gone out into the world",* verse 2 *"Hereby know ye the spirit of God: Every spirit that confesseth that Jesus Chris is come in the flesh is of God":* In Jeremiah 23:21 *"I have not sent these prophets, yet they ran: I have not spoken to them, yet they prophesied."* Receiving a word that God has not spoken will turn out awfully bad, it can make you sick, even kill you. God will always speak to the person first. Then God will send someone with the same word that God had spoken to that person, or awfully close to the word. When God speaks it will resonate with the person in the spirit and the heart!

Chapter Four:
Prophets Will Contest Sin

Elijah is sent to contest with the prophets of Baal. In 1 Kings 18 verse 1 *"And it came to pass after many days, that the word of the Lord came to Elijah in the third year, saying Go, shew thyself unto Ahab, and I will send rain upon the earth."*

The first thing that takes place is the word of the Lord comes to Elijah, saying show yourself to Ahab. He does not go on his own. He goes at the word of the Lord. He goes with the anointed word that says to him go. When God gives the word it is anointed, and it is powerful. We need to remember that the word has power to perform what and where it is sent to. It must do all that God sent it to accomplish.

Verse 2 *"And Elijah went to shew himself unto Ahab. And there was a sore famine in Samaria."*

Elijah shows himself to Ahab and there is famine! Look at where he went! Samaria! In Hebrew it is Shomron and is the central region of ancient Palestine. Samaria extends about 40 miles from north to south and 35 miles from east to west. It is bounded by the Sea of Galilee on the north and by Judea on the south, on the west was the Mediterranean Sea and on the east the Jordan River, according to the Hebrew Bible. We can see that God picks this place to send the prophet, having instructed what to say. Prophets must allow God to train them the right way. No prophet is his own man! Where God sends and who He sends, He prepares. God will send the prophet to places that the prophet would not think of going. God sends Elijah into the enemies' camp to confront the sins of the enemy.

1 Kings 18 verse 7 *"And as Obadiah was in the way, behold, Elijah met him: and he knew him, and fell on his face, and said, art thou that my lord Elijah?"* Verse 8 *"And he answered him, I am: go, tell thy lord, behold, Elijah is here."* When Elijah tells Obadiah tell thy lord that I am here, Obadiah got shook up in his spirit. You can see for yourself that the power of the word put fear in Obadiah. He is given a direct word from the prophet. He must deliver the message, and he knew better than not to obey Elijah. In verse 7 Obadiah saluted him with great respect, fell on his face, and humbly asked, "art thou my lord Elijah." In answer to him, Elijah transfers the title of honor Obadiah gave him to Ahab: Call him thy lord not me, according to the Matthew Henry Study Bible Commentary.

When God sends the prophet he or she will come with a blessing or a word of judgement. In verse 10 *"As the Lord thy God liveth, there is no nation or kingdom, whither my lord hath sent to seek thee: and when they said, He is not there, he took an oath of the kingdom and nation, that they found thee not."* Ahab did not know what trouble he was getting himself into. Ahab sends his soldiers out looking for the prophet Elijah. Ahab does not know the surprise that God has for him. When a nation and its government is in sin God will send His prophets to deal with that nation, its government, and the sin that is there. In Daniel chapter 2:21 *"And he changeth the times and the seasons: he removeth kings, and setteth up kings: he giveth wisdom unto the wise, and knowledge to them that know understanding."* In this verse there is a lot of wisdom and knowledge, God is the one who places and removes!

To summarize what we have learned:

1. Show yourself to Ahab.
2. When God gives the word it is anointed.
3. The word has power.
4. The word will do all that God sent it to do.
5. God picks the place, and what the prophet will say.
6. God will send the prophet into places that he would not think of going.
7. God sends Elijah into the enemies' camp to confront the sins of the enemy.

The prophet must always be in prayer to hear what God is speaking. The prophet will always move at the right time and will not move until he hears from God. God will always show up at the right time. Timing is especially important! Never go where God is not sending you. God will always let you know when to move and when not to. Remember Israel moved when the cloud moved. Verse 21 "And Elijah came unto all the people, and said, How long halt ye between two opinions? If the Lord be God, follow him: but if Baal, then follow him. And the people answered him not a word."

We can see very clearly that the people did not want to answer. This shows that there must be sin that has to be dealt with. The people must come to repent and reform, and then they can look for the judgment to be removed. Elijah had to face 850 false prophets. I would recommend reading 1 KINGS 18, so that you can get a clear picture of what is going on. You will see God at work through His prophet Elijah. Notice what Elijah tells the people about having two opinions, "if the Lord be God, follow him, but if Baal then follow him, they, would not answer." They knew that they were in sin. That is why they kept their mouths shut. What Elijah was telling the people was that they could not worship two gods. Going into the enemies' camp to give the word of the Lord must be extremely hard. What a situation to be in. But the best part about being sent to the camp of the enemy is that you win. If God is for you who can be against you!

When the Lord speaks to the prophet He speaks directly to the prophet. The prophet must always be ready to move when God says move. Moving in Gods timing is crucial. A shift has taken place in the spirit realm for the prophet to move. Moving in the shift is where the word of God removes everything out of the way for the prophet to operate in the assignment, in the power of the Holy Spirit! No prophet can move without the word. The prophet has the heart of God and the Spirit of God. No prophet should go to the camp of the enemy without being sent and having the word of God to direct them! God is the only way, there is no other way. Do not try to be a Lone Ranger! Prayer is always at the front of every assignment. That is where the word of God will come. Remember that your help comes from God! The prophet must always trust in God and God alone.

Always remember when you are not sure pray that you get a clear understanding from God. He will always lead you in the right direction. Always have your Bible with you! Always take your time. You do not have to rush. There is going to be a process to go through. God will never send a prophet out, without being trained.

Chapter Five:
Only a Prophet Can Train a Prophet

> 1 KINGS 19:16 *"And Jehu the son of Nimshi shalt thou anoint to be king over Israel: and Elisha the son of Shaphat of Abelmeholah shalt thou anoint to be prophet in thy room."*

The training of a prophet is very rigorous, and the prophet is always in training. When the person is called to the office of the prophet, that is the start of the training.

The training starts with the voice of God. God does the calling. No man can do the calling for the office of the prophet. Should there be a senior prophet who has the word of the Lord to reveal the call to that person? A call on the life of a person only comes from God. We should always remember that God will always speak to the person who He is calling. Being called does not mean that you can go out on your own. What it does mean, is that you heard God call.

Let us look at verse 16 where God tells Elijah, that Elisha shall be prophet in thy room. This is the beginning of the training of Elisha, to prepare him for the office of the prophet Elijah. Here is where Elijah gets his direct instruction from God for the training of Elisha. When God speaks, He speaks directly to Elijah! Elijah will now act as he has been spoken to by God. This is not do as I want. This is do what God has said to do. When God speaks, we have to remember that God is speaking from the throne room of heaven. Now that the word is being released, it will travel, down from heaven to earth, to the person that it is intended for. What we are seeing is the word coming in power to do what it is intended to do. Without receiving the word there is no movement. For any movement to take place there must be a word from God. The movement of the word creates power. It is in the word coming forth. The word attaches itself to where it is being sent, be it a person, a nation, or a city.

The training for Elisha is to follow Elijah and learn from his spiritual father. Elisha is going to learn the office of the prophet, by direct observation of Elijah. He is going to learn from the prophet, not from anyone else. No person being called to the office of the prophet is going to learn from a pastor unless that pastor is also a prophet. No one can train a prophet better than a prophet. God tells Elijah to anoint Elisha. This is very, important. Why? Because without the anointing there is no sending, and without training there is no sending. God will not send one out on an assignment without being anointed or trained for an assignment. A professional in sports must train to be the best at what they do. Training starts early for any person that has the passion for what they want to become. So, it is with God and the person that He puts His hand upon. Being called is part of who you are going to be for God!

Before anyone can be used of God, they must learn how to serve! One has, to serve in the capacity that they are called to. Elisha served Elijah for eight years before he learns that he is being prepared to replace his spiritual father. How did Elisha serve Elijah? He served his spiritual father by cleaning his clothes, cooking for him, and doing other things. There is no easy way to be a prophet! It takes time to know a person, especially a prophet. I have heard people say, I want to be a prophet, but they do not weigh the cost of becoming a prophet. When one says that they want to be like a person and do what that person does, they better know that there is a cost that comes with it. For anything that a person wants in life, they need to know the cost.

God knows the timing of your life and ministry that He has for you. Elisha did not run ahead of himself, he followed Elijah and learned from him. I am sure that Elisha had a lot of questions on why he had to serve Elijah, why he had to do certain things that he did for Elijah. Elisha knew that he was called to follow and not to lead. You need to learn how to be a servant before you can lead. Elisha was not poor, he was wealthy, he had twelve oxen! Being a servant was undoubtedly a new experience for him, but it was the pathway to becoming the leader when Elijah was gone.

Training to be a prophet is not easy. In training, you learn obedience, knowing when to move and when to stay. Will you make mistakes? Yes, you will. That is why you are learning. Discipline is important for growing in the prophetic. Training makes you sharp and not dull.

In James 1:19 it reads, *"wherefore, my beloved brethren, let every man be swift to hear, slow to speak, slow to wrath."* Training will sharpen your ear gate and senses. Be slow to speak and swift to hear. This will help you in your discernment.

There is no greater training than that which comes from the Holy Spirit, and the prophet that God puts you under.

To summarize what we have learned:

1. There is no greater training than from the Holy Spirit, and the prophet that God puts you under.
2. Discipline is particularly important.
3. Training makes you sharp and not dull.
4. God tells Elijah to anoint Elisha.
5. No anointing, no sending.
6. The training of a prophet is rigorous, and the prophet is always in training.
7. The training will start with the voice of God.
8. The training for Elisha is to follow Elijah and learn from his spiritual father.

9. Be slow to speak and swift to hear.
10. Training to be a prophet is not easy.
11. God knows the timing of your life and ministry.
12. Elisha did not run ahead of himself.

Timing has a lot to do with training and sending. You do not want to move before the right time. God works in time and out of time and is always on time. We must be patient and accept Gods timing. In the waiting, we are being formed to become what God wills in our life. There is a process that is taking place! An old saying is that you must crawl before you can walk. Be patient! I know what I am saying because I had to go through the same process. To become the best in what you do, you must work at it until you finish. Always remember that you must train in whatever you want to be. Practice is what makes anyone better at what they want to be. No one gets a free pass; if you do not put the work in, you will never get what they want. Nothing is free. No one can ask to be a millionaire if they do not learn what it takes to be a millionaire. Studying is always a part of the process that we must go through. The big question is are you willing to go through the process. Never judge a book until you read the book! Remember God is the one that calls and the one that gives the assignment.

Chapter Six:
The Transfer of the Mantle

We are going to look at the transfer of the mantle of Elijah to Elisha. Why did God direct Elijah to Elisha, and God did not direct Elisha to Elijah. Let us look at 1 Kings 19:16 *"And Jehu the son of Nimshi shalt thou anoint to be king over Israel: and Elisha the son of Shaphat of Abelmeholah shalt thou anoint to be prophet in thy room."* I will now break the verse into part B of verse 16.

"And Elisha the son of Shaphat of Abelmeholah shalt thou anoint to be prophet in thy room." I must go to verse 17, so we can get the whole picture.

1 Kings 19:17 *"...him that escapeth the sword of Hazael shall Jehu slay and him that escapeth from the sword of Jehu shall Elisha slay."* This is when Elijah starts his journey to transfer his mantle to Elisha. Elijah did not set out to look for Elisha. God set him on a path where he would find Elisha. God has a way of doing things. God has a plan, and His plan works all the time. God is the best strategist in the world.

Verse 19 *"So he departed thence, and found Elisha the son of Shaphat, who was plowing with twelve yokes of oxen before him, and he with the twelfth: and Elijah passed by him and cast his mantle upon him."*

Prophets were known for wearing mantles as a sign of their calling from God (1 Kings 19:13). The prophet Samuel wore a mantle (1 Samuel 15:27). The prophet Elijah "threw his cloak around [Elisha]" as a symbol of Elijah's ministry being passed on to Elisha. The prophet's mantle was an indication of his authority and responsibility as God's chosen spokesman (2 Kings 2:8). Elisha was not confused as to what Elijah was doing, for the putting on the mantle made Elisha's election clear.

Some theologians see the mantle as a symbol of the Holy Spirit. For example, in 2 Kings 2:14 Elisha takes the mantle that had "fallen" from Elijah. This is similar to how Jesus received the Spirit "descending" on Him at his baptism (Matthew 3:16). The mantle served the practical purpose of keeping people warm and protecting them from the elements. It also served a symbolic purpose. In the case of the prophets it showed they were wrapped in God's authority. Like all imagery in the Old Testament, the mantle presents a visible representation of a New Testament principle. The mantle can be seen as a symbol of the anointing of the Holy Spirit which God so graciously gives to all Christians, the people of His choosing (1 Thessalonians 1:5-6, 1 Peter 2:9). www.gotquestions.org.

When was the mantle of Elijah passed on to Elisha? The mantle was passed to Elisha when Elijah walked by and cast his mantle on Elisha. Elijah is referred to as a power prophet. When his mantle hit Elisha, the ministry was passed on to Elisha. Power was passed on, miracles, signs and wonders included. When God told Elijah to anoint Elisha in his room, all that was in the room would be passed on to Elisha. One of the most important lessons that young prophets need to learn is to be still and know. Elisha understood what was going on. The question that needs to be asked is are you willing to be a student of the Holy Spirit?

It was years before Elisha started his ministry. He did not move ahead of God nor his teacher and spiritual father. He knew that there was a lot to learn. Becoming a prophet is not easy! It takes years. God does not perfect anyone quickly like a dish in a microwave oven. Prophets are not instant. They are made in the back side of the desert. The desert is the training ground for all who are called to the prophets' ministry. The desert is hot, grueling, and lonely. Prophets are not made around people or noise that can distract them from their training. In receiving the mantle, you will need to stay in training and not leave until the training is complete.

There are two things to learn in verse 16 and 17. The first being that Elisha is going to be the prophet in Elijah's room, and will use the sword. This does not take place right away; he must be taught how to use the sword. He does not become prophet in the room of Elijah right away, he must train. If you are looking for an easy way out of training, it is not going to work. There is much to learn about what it takes to be in the prophet's ministry. In verse 20, we see how Elisha begins to minister to Elijah. Elisha submits himself to Elijah and to the training that is ahead of him. Elijah did not tell Elisha to submit himself to him! He or she that is called to the ministry of the prophet will have to learn to submit to their spiritual father or mother.

Do not think that you are the only prophet. There are others that are being called to the prophet's ministry. They are also in training and want to do what God has called them to do. Being patient is going to be at the fore front of the call to the prophet's ministry, and to other ministries. Being called to ministry is not a luxury. Be yourself and not like anyone else. Being you is going to be great. Get your own style, remember that you are unique. God did not make anyone else like you. He made you and you, alone. Follow the blueprint that you have been taught and you will be ok.

To summarize what we have learned:

1. Prophets were known for wearing mantles as a sign of their calling from God.
2. The prophet's mantle was an indication of his authority and responsibility as God's chosen spokesman.
3. Elisha was not confused as to what Elijah was doing. The putting on of his mantle made his election clear.
4. Some theologians see the mantle as a symbol of the Holy Spirit.

5. The mantle was passed to Elisha when Elijah went by and cast his mantle on Elisha.
6. Elijah is referred to as a power prophet.
7. Becoming a prophet is not easy!
8. The mantle served a symbolic purpose, showing they were wrapped in God's authority.

One of the lessons learned was to pray and ask God what spirit of the prophet He had placed on me. It is important for anyone who is called to the prophet's ministry to learn of that prophet. If you do not know that prophet's ministry, you will not know what he or she did. You must know the office of the prophet and the person as prophet. I would recommend that you study all the prophets. You learn a lot by studying who they were and where they came from. Moses passed his mantle on to Joshua! It is especially important that spiritual parents pass their mantles on to the next generation. Sons and daughters should stay under the spiritual parents that God gives them. When a son or a daughter moves before their time, they will lose the timing of God. God works in our time and prepares us to move in His time! The mantle is a gift from God, and He knows who to place it on. He does not place the mantle on just anyone. He places it on the right person! Ask yourself if are you ready to take the next step in your training? Do you want the transfer of the mantle? If so, then learn what it takes to get the mantle. Stay still until Gods appointed time!

Chapter Seven:
Elisha's Request for the Double Portion of the Spirit of Elijah

"And it came to pass, when they were gone over, that Elijah said unto Elisha, ask what I shall do for thee, before I be taken away from thee. And Elisha said, I pray thee, let a double portion of thy spirit be upon me." [2 Kings 2:9]

"And he said, Thou hast asked a hard thing: nevertheless, if thou see me when I am taken from thee, it shall be so unto thee, but if not, it shall not be so." [2 Kings 2:10]

"And it came to pass, as they still went on, and talked, that, behold, there appeared a chariot of fire, and horses of fire, and parted them both asunder; and Elijah went up by a whirlwind into heaven." [2 Kings 2:11]

"And Elisha saw it, and he cried, My father, my father, the chariot of Israel, and the horsemen thereof. And he saw him no more: and he took hold of his own clothes and rent them in two pieces." [2 Kings 2:12]

"He took up also the mantle of Elijah that fell from him, and went back, and stood by the bank of Jordan;" [2 Kings 2:13]

"And he took the mantle of Elijah that fell from him, and smote the waters, and said, Where is the LORD GOD of Elijah? And when he also had smitten the waters, they parted hither and thither: and Elisha went over." [2 Kings 2:14]

"And when the sons of the prophets which were to view at Jericho saw him, they said, The spirit of Elijah doth rest on Elisha. And they came to meet him, and bowed themselves to the ground before him." [2 Kings 2:15]

Elijah is getting ready for his departure, and he asked Elisha what he would like for him to do for him? Elisha's reply is, to give him a double portion of his spirit. Elijah's reply is that he was asking a hard thing, but if he saw Elijah being taken it would be so. Did Elisha ask for a double portion because Elisha knew the scriptures taught about the double blessing? The Old Testament teaches about the birthright, or the inheritance that the oldest son receives.

Deuteronomy 21:17 reads, *"He shall acknowledge the firstborn, the son of the unloved, by giving him a double portion that he has, for he is the first fruits of his strength."* The right of the firstborn is his. This shows that Elisha knew the scriptures well. Elisha knew how to ask for the double portion, he knew that he would need the double portion of Elijah for his life and ministry. Elisha had 28 miracles in his ministry, and Elijah had 14. This shows that Elisha was taught very well by Elijah.

Hannah's husband gave her a double portion because of his love for her and because she did not have children. [1 Samuel 1:5]

> *"God tells Israel, For your shame ye shall have double, and for confusion they shall rejoice in their portion: therefore in their land they shall possess the double: everlasting joy shall be unto them."* [Isaiah 61:7]

Elisha sees Elijah being taken away by the chariot of Israel and the horsemen. Before this takes place the scripture says the horses parted them both asunder, meaning that they were separated. The separation took place so that Elisha would not go with Elijah. God wanted Elisha to stay and fill the room of Elijah. The next thing that takes place is that Elijah drops his mantle and Elisha picks it up. Here the complete transfer takes place. For the ministry of Elisha to begin Elijah had to leave. Never be too quick to move!

Elisha has the mantle, and he goes back the way that he came with Elijah. He stands by the bank of the Jordan; he takes the mantle of Elijah and strikes the waters just as Elijah did. He then says "where is the God of Elijah?" When he hit the waters, they parted. He did just as Elijah had done before him. He then crosses over to the other side.

Let us go back some. The sons of the prophets were making fun of Elisha. They were saying that Elijah was going to be leaving. Elisha replied, yes, I know, hold your peace. This shows that there was a spirit of jealousy on the other prophets. They did not know what was going to take place. When they saw that Elisha struck the waters just like Elijah did, they were surprised. Then they said that the spirit of Elijah rested on Elisha and they bowed themselves to the ground before him. They reverenced Elisha and the spirit of Elijah on him.

Is it biblical for a double portion? Yes, it is. The bible has 27 verses on double (KJV), 6 verses on double-edged (NIV), 3 on double-minded (NIV), 1 double-pronged (NIV) and 1 doubly (NIV).

The bible also has 73 verses on position. Now let us look at the word position and what it has to do with Elisha. Elisha was in the right position when Elijah found him. Elisha is at the right place so Elijah could place his mantle on him. Position has a lot to do with anyone in whom God is going to work with and work through. If Elisha were not in the proper position, he would have delayed his calling. In the position that Elijah finds Elisha is when the mantle is going to be transferred. Now God begins the work in Elisha. God does not begin the work on the outside. God begins the work on the inside, then He shows it on the outside. Even when you are working, they put you in the position of the job that you will do. Working for God is not easy! If you think that it will be easy to work in the Kingdom, think again!

Having a mantle placed on the person that God calls, means that they have much responsibility. For anyone that wants the mantle of the person that they are under, you will have to show God that you are the one that can carry the mantle with honor and respect. Taking up the mantle means that you are not your own anymore, you are saying that God oversees your life. The placing of the mantle means that the person that gets the mantle will honor and respect the mantle and will honor God. The mantle is sacred to God!

A prophet is always in prayer to hear the heartbeat of the Father. The prophet is always ready to hear from God. The prophet is ready to move at a moment's notice when God says go to the next place. Elisha was prepared physically, but he had to be prepared spiritually. There are a lot of Elijah's and a lot of Elisha's waiting to be trained.

To summarize what we have learned:

1. Elijah is getting ready for his departure.
2. To give him a double portion of his spirit.
3. Elisha knew the scriptures taught about the double portion.
4. In The old testament, it teaches about the birthright or inheritance that the oldest son receives.
5. The right of the first born is his.
6. The separation took place so that Elisha would not go with Elijah.
7. God wanted Elisha to stay and fill the room of Elijah.
8. Elijah drops his mantle and Elisha picks it up.
9. Never be too quick to move.
10. Elisha was in the right position when Elijah found him.
11. Taking up the mantle means that you are not your own anymore, you are saying that God oversees your life.
12. The mantle is sacred to God!
13. Elisha was already prepared physically, but he had to be prepared spiritually.
14. Elisha knew how to ask for the double portion, he knew that he would need the double portion of the spirit of Elijah for his life and ministry.

It is important that the prophet have a double portion of the prophet that God has put them under. Learning about the double portion is important. Never leave from under your covering unless God tells you so. Remember, Israel did not move when the cloud did not move. Young prophets have a tendency of moving before their time of training is over. An old saying that my mother would tell me, Rome was not built in a day, but it went down in one day. Keep in mind what is at stake. God is building a ministry in you, to bring out of you, at the right time. God is a God of perfect timing. He is always on time!

Do not be like the young prophet that was sent on an assignment and because of disobedience a lion killed him; obedience is always at the top of any assignment that is given to anyone from God. Getting the mantle or having the mantle will always require obedience to God and to the spiritual parents that God gives to the young prophet in training. You cannot get what you want without training for it. Every prophet goes through training to learn the heart of the Father. Keep your eyes on the Lord at all times! When you do not know the answer ask and you will get the answer. If you are seeking the double portion of your spiritual father or mother learn how to get the attention of the heavenly Father and when it is time, He will place it on you. There is no other way! Seek and you shall find, knock and the door of knowledge and wisdom shall be opened unto you. Remember that God loves you! It is time to move on to greater things in your life and ministry. There are some things that you will say and some that you will keep between you and God. Always remember to seek the heart of the Father!

Chapter Eight:
What Are the Characteristics of a True Prophet?

A prophet is one who speaks for another, or someone who lends his voice to another. The major purpose of these servants – prophets – was to declare God's heart to His people by piercing the hearts of his people that they might return to His ways. Let us look at the characteristics of a true prophet.

1. Worshipper

Definition: Veneration (honor, esteem, worship), glorification, elevate, enhance, dignify, hail and to exalt.

> Judges 5:1-5. The Song of Deborah. On that day Deborah and Barak son of Abinoam sang this song:*"When the princes in Israel take the lead, When the people willingly offer themselves – praise the Lord! Hear this, you kings! Listen, you rulers! I will sing to the Lord, I will sing; I will make music to the Lord, the God of Israel. O Lord, when you went out from Seir, when you marched from the land of Edom, the earth shook, the heavens poured, the clouds poured down water. The mountains quaked before the Lord, the One of Sinai, before the Lord, the God of Israel."*

> Daniel 2:19–23 *"…Then Daniel praised the God of heaven and said: "Praise be to the name of God for ever and ever; wisdom and power are his. He changes times and seasons; he sets up kings and deposes them. He gives wisdom to the wise and knowledge to the discerning. He reveals deep and hidden things; he knows what lies in darkness, and light dwells with him. I thank and praise you, O God of my fathers: You have given me wisdom and power, you have made known to me what we asked of you, you have made known to us the dream of the king."*

2. Intercessor

Definition: A mediator; one who interposes between parties at variance, with a view to reconcile them; one who pleads in behalf of another.

> 1 Kings 13:6. *"Then the king said to the man of God, intercede with the Lord your God and pray for me that my hand may be restored. So the man of God interceded with the Lord, and the king's hand was restored and became as it was before."*

Habakkuk 2:1. *"I will stand at my watch and station myself on the ramparts; I will look to see what he will say to me, and what answer I am to give to his complaint."*

3. Meekness: as in all the characteristics, Jesus is our perfect example

Definition: humble and submissive, piously gentle in nature.

Gentleness: mild or kind – in temperament, moderate, kindly, tender, thoughtful, gracious, compassionate.

Philippians 2:1-5. *Imitating Christ's Humility. "Therefore if you have any encouragement from being united with Christ, if any comfort from his love, if any common sharing in the Spirit, if any tenderness and compassion, then make my joy complete by being like – minded, having the same love, being one in spirit and of one mind. Do nothing out of selfish ambition or vain conceit. Rather, in humility value others above yourselves, not looking to your own interests but each of you to the interests of the others."*

In your relationships with one another, have the same mindset as Christ Jesus.

4. Knows the word of God, therefore knows God

Definition – Knows: have in the mind, have learned, be able to recall (knows what to do), be aware of.

1 Samuel 15:22. *"But Samuel replied: Does the Lord delight in burnt offerings and sacrifices as much as in obeying the voice of the Lord? To obey is better than sacrifice, and to heed is better than the fat of rams."*

5. Forgiving:

Definition – Forgive: cease to feel angry or resentful, pardon, overlook, clear, acquit, absolve, acquittal, allowance.

Numbers 12:13. *"Moses cried out to the Lord, O God please heal her!"*

6. Filled with the Holy Spirit

Definition – Filled: occupy completely, spread over or through, pervade, take over.

John 6:63. *"The Spirit gives life; the flesh counts for nothing. The words I have spoken to you are spirit and they are life."*

1 Corinthians 2:14. *"The man without the Spirit does not accept the things that come from the Spirit of God, for they are foolishness to him, and he cannot understand them, because they are spiritually discerned."*

John 14:16-17. *"And I will ask the Father, and he will give you another Counselor to be with you forever -- The Spirit of truth. The world cannot accept him because it neither sees him nor knows him. But you know him, for he lives with you and will be in you."*

John 16:7. *"But I tell you the truth: It is for your good that I am going away. Unless I go away, the Counselor will not come to you, but if I go, I will send him to you."*

7. Fearless – he/she fears God and not man.

Definition – Courageous: brave, bold, intrepid (fearless, very brave, unafraid) daring, audacious (daring, bold, confident).

2 Kings 3:14-15. *"Elisha said, As surely as the Lord Almighty lives, whom I serve, if I did not have respect for the presence of Jehoshaphat king of Judah, I would not look at you or even notice you. But now bring me a harpist. "While they were playing, the hand of the Lord came upon Elisha."*

Jeremiah 1:17. *"Get yourself ready! Stand up and say to them whatever I command you. Do not be terrified by them, or will terrify you before them."*

8. Trusts God

Definition – Trust: firm belief in the reliability, truth, or strength of a person or thing, confident expectation.

Habakkuk 3:17–19. *"Though the fig tree does not bud and there are no grapes on the vines, though the olive crop fails and the fields produce no food, though there are no sheep in the pen and no cattle in the stalls, Yet I will rejoice in the Lord, I will be joyful in God my Savior. The Sovereign Lord is my strength; he makes my feet like feet of a deer, he enables me to go on the heights. For the director of music. On my stringed instruments."*

9. Pure heart

Definition: Pure, unalloyed (uncontaminated, clear, unalloyed (unmixed, unblended, unadulterated, uncorrupted, clear, purified).

Matthew 5:8. *"Blessed are the pure in heart, for they will see God."*

Psalm 12:6. *"And the words of the Lord are flawless, like silver refined in a furnace of clay, purified seven times."*

Deuteronomy 6:5–7. *"Love the Lord your God with all your heart and with your soul and with all your strength. These commandments that I give you today are to be upon your hearts. Impress them on your children. Talk about them when you sit at home and when you walk along the road, when you lie down and when you get up."*

10. Integrity

Definition: Integrity: moral uprightness, honesty, wholeness, soundness, decency, honor, totality, whole, entirety, completeness, (sum total).

2 Kings 5:26-27. *"But Elisha said to him, "was not my spirit with you when the man got down from his chariot to meet you? Is this the time to take money, or to accept clothes, olive groves, vineyards, flocks, herds, or menservants and maidservants"? Naaman's leprosy will cling to you and to your descendants forever. "Then Gehazi went from Elisha's presence and he was leprous as white as snow."*

Daniel 6:3-5. *"Now Daniel so distinguished himself among the administrators and the satraps by his exceptional qualities that the king planned to set him over the whole kingdom. At this, the administrators and the satraps tried to find grounds for charges against Daniel in his conduct of government affairs, but they were unable to do so. They could find no corruption in him, because he was trustworthy and neither corrupt nor negligent. Finally these men said, "We will never find any basis for charges against this man Daniel unless it has something to do with the law of his God."*

11. Exercise discretion and strong discernment

Definition: Discretion: freedom to act and think as one wishes usually within legal limits, tact, diplomacy, delicacy.

Discernment: good judgment or insight, perceive clearly with the mind or the senses.

Acts 16:17–18. *"She followed Paul and the rest of us, shouting, "These men are servants of the Most High God, who are telling you the way to be saved." 18 She kept this up for many days. Finally Paul became so annoyed that he turned around and said to the spirit, "In the name of Jesus Christ I command you to come out of her!" At that moment the spirit left her."*

Proverbs 10:19. *"Sin is not ended by multiplying words, but the prudent hold their tongues."*

Proverbs 30:5-6. *"Every word of God is flawless; he is a shield to those who take refuge in him. Do not add to his words, or he will rebuke you and prove you a liar."*

12. Have no agenda but God's agenda.

Definition: Agenda: a list of things to be dealt with or especially an underlying motivation.

>Proverbs 3:5-6. *"Trust in the Lord with all your heart and lean not on your own understanding; in all your ways submit to him, and he will make your paths straight."*

>Luke 10:27. *"He answered, "'Love the Lord your God with all your heart and with all your soul and with all your strength and with all your mind'[a]; and, 'Love your neighbor as yourself.'"*

>Matthew 6:31-34. *So do not worry, saying, 'What shall we eat?' or 'What shall we drink?' or 'What shall we wear?' For the pagans run after all these things, and your heavenly Father knows that you need them. But seek first his kingdom and his righteousness, and all these things will be given to you as well. Therefore do not worry about tomorrow, for tomorrow will worry about itself. Each day has enough trouble of its own.*

>Romans 14:7-18. *"For none of us lives for ourselves alone, and none of us dies for ourselves alone. If we live, we live for the Lord; and if we die, we die for the Lord. So, whether we live or die, we belong to the Lord. For this very reason, Christ died and returned to life so that he might be the Lord of both the dead and the living.*

>*You, then, why do you judge your brother or sister? Or why do you treat them with contempt? For we will all stand before God's judgment seat. It is written:"'As surely as I live,' says the Lord,'every knee will bow before me; every tongue will acknowledge God. So then, each of us will give an account of ourselves to God.'"*

Therefore let us stop passing judgment on one another. Instead, make up your mind not to put any stumbling block or obstacle in the way of a brother or sister. I am convinced, being fully persuaded in the Lord Jesus, that nothing is unclean in itself. But if anyone regards something as unclean, then for that person it is unclean. If your brother or sister is distressed because of what you eat, you are no longer acting in love. Do not by your eating destroy someone for whom Christ died. Therefore do not let what you know is good be spoken of as evil. For the kingdom of God is not a matter of eating and drinking, but of righteousness, peace and joy in the Holy Spirit, because anyone who serves Christ in this way is pleasing to God and receives human approval.

>Romans 5:5. *"And hope does not put us to shame, because God's love has been poured out into our hearts through the Holy Spirit, who has been given to us."*

13. Obedient

Definition: submissive, dutiful (following the law), compliant, respectful.

> Ezekiel 24:15-18. *"The word of the LORD came to me: "Son of man, with one blow I am about to take away from you the delight of your eyes. Yet do not lament or weep or shed any tears. Groan quietly; do not mourn for the dead. Keep your turban fastened and your sandals on your feet; do not cover your mustache and beard or eat the customary food of mourners." So I spoke to the people in the morning, and in the evening my wife died. The next morning I did as I had been commanded."*

> Jeremiah 16:1-4. *"Then the word of the LORD came to me: "You must not marry and have sons or daughters in this place." For this is what the LORD says about the sons and daughters born in this land and about the women who are their mothers and the men who are their fathers: "They will die of deadly diseases. They will not be mourned or buried but will be like dung lying on the ground. They will perish by sword and famine, and their dead bodies will become food for the birds and the wild animals."*

14. They are good listeners

Definition: - Good: having the right desired qualities

Listeners: make an effort to hear, take notice; heed.

> 1 Samuel 3:10. *"The LORD came and stood there, calling as at the other times, "Samuel! Samuel!" Then Samuel said, "Speak, for your servant is listening."*

15. They have wisdom

Definition: Wisdom: The right use or exercise of knowledge; the choice of laudable ends, and of the best means to accomplish them.

Prudence is the exercise of sound judgment in avoiding evils; wisdom is the exercise of sound judgment either in avoiding evils or attempting good. Prudence then is a species, of which wisdom is the genus, discernment, reason, insight, common sense.

> John 16:13. *"But when he, the Spirit of truth, comes, he will guide you into all the truth. He will not speak on his own; he will speak only what he hears, and he will tell you what is yet to come."*

> Genesis 41:37-38. *"The plan seemed good to Pharaoh and to all his officials. 38 So Pharaoh asked them, "Can we find anyone like this man, one in whom is the spirit of God?"*

16. Prophets are fearless and strong in resolve

Definitions: Fearless: courageous, brave, bold, intrepid, daring, audacious.

Strong: solid, sturdy, substantial, stout, tough, sound, well-built, reinforced.

Resolved: make up one's mind, decide firmly, firm mental decision or intention.

1 John 4:13-21. *"This is how we know that we live in him and he in us: He has given us of his Spirit. And we have seen and testify that the Father has sent his Son to be the Savior of the world. If anyone acknowledges that Jesus is the Son of God, God lives in them and they in God. And so we know and rely on the love God has for us. God is love. Whoever lives in love lives in God, and God in them. This is how love is made complete among us so that we will have confidence on the day of judgment: In this world we are like Jesus. There is no fear in love. But perfect love drives out fear, because fear has to do with punishment. The one who fears is not made perfect in love. We love because he first loved us. Whoever claims to love God yet hates a brother or sister is a liar. For whoever does not love their brother and sister, whom they have seen, cannot love God, whom they have not seen. And he has given us this command: Anyone who loves God must also love their brother and sister."*

John 15:1-17. *"I am the true vine, and my Father is the gardener. He cuts off every branch in me that bears no fruit, while every branch that does bear fruit he prunes so that it will be even more fruitful. You are already clean because of the word I have spoken to you. Remain in me, as I also remain in you. No branch can bear fruit by itself; it must remain in the vine. Neither can you bear fruit unless you remain in me.*

"I am the vine; you are the branches. If you remain in me and I in you, you will bear much fruit; apart from me you can do nothing. If you do not remain in me, you are like a branch that is thrown away and withers; such branches are picked up, thrown into the fire and burned. If you remain in me and my words remain in you, ask whatever you wish, and it will be done for you. This is to my Father's glory, that you bear much fruit, showing yourselves to be my disciples.

"As the Father has loved me, so have I loved you. Now remain in my love. If you keep my commands, you will remain in my love, just as I have kept my Father's commands and remain in his love. I have told you this so that my joy may be in you and that your joy may be complete. My command is this: Love each other as I have loved you. Greater love has no one than this: to lay down one's life for one's friends. You are my friends if you do what I command. I no longer call you servants, because a servant does not know his master's business. Instead, I have called you friends, for everything that I learned from my Father I have made

known to you. You did not choose me, but I chose you and appointed you so that you might go and bear fruit—fruit that will last—and so that whatever you ask in my name the Father will give you. This is my command: Love each other."

Joshua 1:13-18. *"Remember the command that Moses the servant of the LORD gave you after he said, 'The LORD your God will give you rest by giving you this land.' Your wives, your children and your livestock may stay in the land that Moses gave you east of the Jordan, but all your fighting men, ready for battle, must cross over ahead of your fellow Israelites. You are to help them until the LORD gives them rest, as he has done for you, and until they too have taken possession of the land the LORD your God is giving them. After that, you may go back and occupy your own land, which Moses the servant of the LORD gave you east of the Jordan toward the sunrise."*

Then they answered Joshua, "Whatever you have commanded us we will do, and wherever you send us we will go. Just as we fully obeyed Moses, so we will obey you. Only may the LORD your God be with you as he was with Moses. Whoever rebels against your word and does not obey it, whatever you may command them, will be put to death. Only be strong and courageous!"

Nehemiah 8:10. *"Nehemiah said, "Go and enjoy choice food and sweet drinks, and send some to those who have nothing prepared. This day is holy to our Lord. Do not grieve, for the joy of the LORD is your strength."*

17. Prophets fight for others, but they do not defend themselves. They let God defend them instead.

Definitions: Fight: contend or struggle, strive determinedly to achieve something, to overcome.

Defend: resist an attack on, protect, support, or uphold, shield, champion.

Jeremiah 15:20-21. *"I will make you a wall to this people, a fortified wall of bronze; they will fight against you but will not overcome you, for I am with you to rescue and save you," declares the Lord. "I will save you from the hands of the wicked and deliver you from the grasp of the cruel."*

18. Prophets have a kingly mindset, great boldness, strong, and a completely confident focus on the Lord Jesus and His word. They only let God change the instructions.

Some people might say, "You have a big head." As a prophet, it is true! Christ Jesus is your Head! He is going to say fantastic things through you; God is faithful. They will surely happen if you obey Him. Some might also say, "You've lost your mind." They are right! You have lost your mind and now have the mind of Christ.

1 Corinthians 2:15-16. *"The person with the Spirit makes judgments about all things, but such a person is not subject to merely human judgments, for, "Who has known the mind of the Lord so as to instruct him?" But we have the mind of Christ."*

Ephesians 4:14-16. *"Then we will no longer be infants, tossed back and forth by the waves, and blown here and there by every wind of teaching and by the cunning and craftiness of people in their deceitful scheming. Instead, speaking the truth in love, we will grow to become in every respect the mature body of him who is the head, that is, Christ. From him the whole body, joined and held together by every supporting ligament, grows and builds itself up in love, as each part does its work."*

2 Corinthians 11:3. *"But I am afraid that just as Eve was deceived by the serpent's cunning, your minds may somehow be led astray from your sincere and pure devotion to Christ."*

Philippians 4:6-8. *"Do not be anxious about anything, but in every situation, by prayer and petition, with thanksgiving, present your requests to God. And the peace of God, which transcends all understanding, will guard your hearts and your minds in Christ Jesus. Finally, brothers and sisters, whatever is true, whatever is noble, whatever is right, whatever is pure, whatever is lovely, whatever is admirable—if anything is excellent or praiseworthy—think about such things."*

1 Peter 1:13-16. *"Therefore, with minds that are alert and fully sober, set your hope on the grace to be brought to you when Jesus Christ is revealed at his coming. As obedient children, do not conform to the evil desires you had when you lived in ignorance. But just as he who called you is holy, so be holy in all you do; for it is written: "Be holy, because I am holy.""*

2 Corinthians 10:5. *"We demolish arguments and every pretension that sets itself up against the knowledge of God, and we take captive every thought to make it obedient to Christ."*

1 Kings 13:11-18. *Now there was a certain old prophet living in Bethel, whose sons came and told him all that the man of God had done there that day. They also told their father what he had said to the king. Their father asked them, "Which way did he go?" And his sons showed him which road the man of God from Judah had taken. So he said to his sons, "Saddle the donkey for me." And when they had saddled the donkey for him, he mounted it and rode after the man*

of God. He found him sitting under an oak tree and asked, "Are you the man of God who came from Judah?" "I am," he replied. So the prophet said to him, "Come home with me and eat." The man of God said, "I cannot turn back and go with you, nor can I eat bread or drink water with you in this place. 17 I have been told by the word of the LORD: 'You must not eat bread or drink water there or return by the way you came.'" The old prophet answered, "I too am a prophet, as you are. And an angel said to me by the word of the LORD: 'Bring him back with you to your house so that he may eat bread and drink water.'" (But he was lying to him.)"

1 John 4:1. *"Dear friends, do not believe every spirit, but test the spirits to see whether they are from God, because many false prophets have gone out into the world."*

1 Kings 18:19-24. *"Now summon the people from all over Israel to meet me on Mount Carmel. And bring the four hundred and fifty prophets of Baal and the four hundred prophets of Asherah, who eat at Jezebel's table. So Ahab sent word throughout all Israel and assembled the prophets on Mount Carmel. Elijah went before the people and said, "How long will you waver between two opinions? If the LORD is God, follow him; but if Baal is God, follow him." But the people said nothing. Then Elijah said to them, "I am the only one of the LORD's prophets left, but Baal has four hundred and fifty prophets. Get two bulls for us. Let Baal's prophets choose one for themselves, and let them cut it into pieces and put it on the wood but not set fire to it. I will prepare the other bull and put it on the wood but not set fire to it. Then you call on the name of your god, and I will call on the name of the LORD. The god who answers by fire—he is God." Then all the people said, "What you say is good."*

1 John 4:1-6. *Dear friends, do not believe every spirit, but test the spirits to see whether they are from God, because many false prophets have gone out into the world. This is how you can recognize the Spirit of God: Every spirit that acknowledges that Jesus Christ has come in the flesh is from God, but every spirit that does not acknowledge Jesus is not from God. This is the spirit of the antichrist, which you have heard is coming and even now is already in the world. You, dear children, are from God and have overcome them, because the one who is in you is greater than the one who is in the world. They are from the world and therefore speak from the viewpoint of the world, and the world listens to them. We are from God, and whoever knows God listens to us; but whoever is not from God does not listen to us. This is how we recognize the Spirit of truth and the spirit of falsehood.*

Study all the scriptures.

Chapter Nine:
A Prophet in the Old Testament

The prophet in the Old Testament was one who was used by God to communicate His message to the world. Prophets were called "seers" because they could see, in the spiritual realm and they could hear God speaking in that spiritual realm, as He gave them insight [1 Samuel 9:9]. Prophets can be divided into the "writing prophets" such as Isaiah, Daniel, Amos, and Malachi, and "non- writing prophets" such as Gad, [1 Samuel 22 : 5], Nathan [1 Chronicles 17:1] and Elijah [1 Kings 18 : 36]. There are some anonymous prophets in the Old Testament, and the unnamed prophet in Judges 6:7-10.

Prophets came from different backgrounds and spoke to different audiences. They had unique styles, and different methods. Most Old Testament prophets' messages were to Israel and other nations sometimes mentioned in the oracles. It was also in connection to the nations that were dealing with Israel. Most prophets of God were men, but in the Old Testament it also mentions prophetesses Miriam [Exodus 15:20], Deborah [Judges 4:4], and Huldah ;2 Kings 22:14].

A prophet is called by God to be a prophet. Isaiah and Ezekiel had visions of the glory of God, that were given by God [Isaiah 6 and Ezekiel 1].

God has a conversation with Jeremiah and tells him, "Before I formed you in the womb I knew you", meaning that before you were born, I set you apart. "I appointed you a prophet to the nations" [Jeremiah 1:5].

The common message is that the word came to the prophet. For example:

Jeremiah 1:2. *"The word of the LORD came to him in the thirteenth year of the reign of Josiah son of Amon king of Judah."*

Ezekiel 1:3. *"...the word of the LORD came to Ezekiel the priest, the son of Buzi, by the Kebar River in the land of the Babylonians. There the hand of the LORD was on him."*

Hosea 1:1. *"The word of the LORD that came to Hosea son of Beeri during the reigns of Uzziah, Jotham, Ahaz and Hezekiah, kings of Judah, and during the reign of Jeroboam son of Jehoash king of Israel."*

Joel 1:1. *"The word of the LORD that came to Joel son of Pethuel."*

Jonah 1:1. *"The word of the LORD came to Jonah son of Amittai."*

Micah 1:1. *"The word of the LORD that came to Micah of Moresheth during the reigns of Jotham, Ahaz and Hezekiah, kings of Judah—the vision he saw concerning Samaria and Jerusalem."*

The prophet was required to deliver God's message accurately. The prophet Micaiah says it well, "As surely as the Lord lives, I can tell [the king] only what the Lord tells me." [1 Kings 22:14]. Jeremiah tried to be silent but found out that he could not [Jeremiah 20:9]. Jonah tried to avoid his responsibility but was corrected [Jonah 1:3-4]. Others like the unnamed prophet from Judah who directly disobeyed God lost their lives for being disobedient to the command of God.

Prophets at times had a unique appearance. Elijah was known for wearing "a garment of hair and a leather belt around his waist" [2 Kings 1:8]. Elijah's mantle which he left for Elisha was also seen as a symbol of the prophetic office [2 Kings 2:13-14]. God tells Ezekiel to shave his head and beard [Ezekiel 5:1]. Other prophets were separated in other ways. All prophets were recognized through whom God spoke.

Prophets at times lived a hard life. For example, Isaiah was sent to people who were hearing, but not having understanding and eventually was murdered. Jezebel, the queen of Israel set out to take the life of Elijah. The life of the prophet was always in danger. One reason was because they did not always bring a favorable word. True prophets will always say what God what tells them. We must remember that God never lies, and a true prophet will not lie. In Luke 11:49 –50, Jesus tells us

"Therefore also said the wisdom of God, I will send them prophets and apostles, and some of them they shall persecute. That the blood of all the prophets, which was shed from the foundation of the world, may be required of this generation."

These are strong words coming from Jesus, using the Old Testament to remind them of what their parents did to the prophets! In Verse 48 He also says, "Truly ye bear witness that ye allow the deeds of your fathers: for they indeed killed them, and ye build their sepulchers." Jesus did not have a problem reminding them of their past and present sins. If you think being a prophet is fun think again, because they are often ridiculed and criticized. God never gives us more than we can bear and knows on whom to place the call of a prophet. He does not place the mantle on just anyone. He places it on the right person.

Prophets in the Old Testament prophesied of the future. At times, the prophecies concerned events that would soon take place.

There are also false prophets that are mentioned in the Old Testament. They were liars who claimed to speak for God, but their intent was to deceive the people of God, for their own interest.

To summarize what we have learned:

1. Prophets had a unique appearance.
2. Elijah's mantle which he left for Elisha.
3. All prophets were recognized through whom God spoke through.
4. Prophets were always in danger.
5. True prophets will always say what God tells them.
6. God never lies.
7. A true prophet will not lie.
8. The life of the prophet was always in danger.
9. God places the mantle on the right person.
10. Other prophets were separated in other ways.

As one being called to the ministry and office of the prophet never think that you are better than any other prophet. Each prophet has his or her own portion, and assignment. Always remember that you are in training! There is always something new to learn! Always remain teachable and respond when God is speaking. Be humble, remember that the fight is not yours, it belongs to God! Never pick a fight that you cannot win, God will pick the fight and He will win the fight. 2 Chronicles 20:15 states,

> *"And he said, Hearken ye, all Judah, and ye inhabitants of Jerusalem, and thou king Jehoshaphat, Thus saith the Lord unto you, Be not afraid nor dismayed by reason of this great multitude; for the battle is not yours, but God's."*

God has always had times and seasons when to go to battle. Moving and doing what God speaks at the right time will always be a win-win. God never loses a battle! Always move in Gods timing. Moving out of His timing will not have good results. Always keep in mind when God is for you who can come against you. Never stop looking up to where your help comes from! Remember that God picked you to do the assignment, and God will complete the assignment with you. God is the blueprint to your assignment. Never tell anyone about your assignment unless God tells you who to share it with. Learning with God and from God, and the Holy Spirit is the best teacher that anyone can have. God will also give you an exceptionally good teacher in the person of your spiritual covering.

Chapter Ten:
Who Is the Prophet in the Bible?

The prophet in the bible is the person who speaks the true word of God to others. According to the Hebrew – Greek Key Word Study Bible (KJV), the word prophet in the English translation comes from the Greek word prophetes which means, one that speaks forth or advocates. In the Old Testament prophets were called seers, because they had spiritual insight and the ability to see into the future.

We find in the Bible that prophets had the ability to teach, and a revelatory role, declaring truth of the word of God on contemporary issues, while also revealing details of the future. For example, Isaiah's ministry touched on the present and the future. When reading the book of Isaiah, we find that he preached very boldly of the corruption in his days.

The prophets have the task to faithfully speak the word of God to the people and to the nations. The prophets, whether old or new, are instrumental in guiding the nation of Israel and establishing the church. The church is built on the foundation of the apostles and the prophets, Jesus Christ himself the chief cornerstone [Ephesians 2:20].

The bible mentions more than 133 prophets. Some may be under the impression that the office of the prophets was filled by men only, such as the 70 elders of Israel [Numbers 11:25]. However, the bible tells us about 16 women prophetesses. Obadiah hid 100 prophets in a cave. God tells Elijah that he has 7000 prophets that have not bowed to Baal [1 Kings 19:18]. This lets us know that pastors should be looking in their ministries to find the prophets God has given them as gifts.

In the time of Elijah and Elisha there was an extremely high level of prophetic activity. There was also a school for training young prophets. [2 Kings 2:5).

God had performed many miracles through Elijah and Elisha [1 Kings 20:36].

John the Baptist was the last Old Testament prophet who prophesied the coming of our Lord Jesus the Christ, fulfilling the prophecies in the Old Testament. [Matthew 3:3].

Included in the early church was the prophets, such as Paul, Ananias who prophesied about Paul's future [Acts 9:10-18]. The bible also speaks of four daughters of Philip who could prophesy [Acts 21:8–9). We must not confuse those that have the gift to prophesy with the ones called to the office of the prophet.

Prophets are sent by God to churches, to nations, to cities and to individuals, with a message from God. Prophets are often despised, and their message not received. In the book of Isaiah, he describes his nation as a rebellious people, deceitful children, unwilling to listen to the instruction of the Lord. They would say to the seers, "See no more visions! And to the prophets, Give us no more visions of what is right! Let us hear pleasant things, prophesy illusions" [Isaiah 30:9-10].

Not everyone that prophesies speaks the true word of God and what God is saying honestly. There are false prophets that claim to speak for God, who are not qualified to speak for the Lord! False prophets are used by the devil to deceive the people of God! The bible tells us that Ahab had 850 false prophets [1 Kings 18:18-19]. The New Testament gives us warning of false prophets. They come in sheep's clothing but are ferocious wolves. The church must watch out for false prophets!

The true prophet of God will be committed to speaking God's truth. He or she will never contradict the true word of God that God has revealed to them. This is the true prophet of God. This is what the true prophet does. He or she will reveal the heart of God as God reveals the word to them. The truth shall set you free from all false words that are released. We must avoid being led astray and we should always try the spirits to see whether they are from God [1 John 4:1].

Prophets must be patient, to hear when God is speaking to them. Being patient will open the portals of heaven. Be faithful in all that God is doing in your life and in the calling that He has called you to. Commit to prayer in everything that God speaks to you, and you will see the blessing of the Lord in your calling. God called you and God will perfect you in the calling. Do not be anxious for nothing! Always be ready to answer God when He calls upon you. Remember that you are always in spiritual warfare. When you are not sure, your best tool will be prayer. God will answer. The prophet is like the cloud, move when the cloud moves and be still when the cloud is still. This is obedience of the true prophet. He moves when God says to move. Being a prophet is not easy! Interacting with Holy Spirit at all times will be the best way to get the guidance and council of God.

To summarize what we have learned:

1. The person called by God to give a specific message to the people of God is a prophet.
2. n the old testament prophets were called seers.
3. They had spiritual insight and the ability to see into the future.
4. Prophets have the ability to teach.
5. Prophets declare the truth of the word of God on contemporary issues.
6. Isaiah's ministry touched on the present and future.
7. Isaiah preached very boldly of the corruption in his days.
8. When God calls you, God will perfect the calling in you.
9. Do not be anxious for anything.

10. Prophets must be patient.
11. Be faithful in all that God is doing in your life and in the calling that He has called you to.
12. The true prophet of God will be committed to speaking God's truth.

Learning who the prophet is in the bible is going to be important to the person who is called to the ministry. This will help the prophet understand the work that God does through him. Remember that God is the one who makes the prophet. The prophet does not make himself. God makes him. For the prophet to know who he is, he must know how God worked with the prophets in the bible. God works differently with each prophet. No two prophets are the same, each one is different. Learning, observing, and listening to the instruction of the teacher, and the Holy Spirit is important!

The real prophet of God has the heart of God and has an ear to hear the voice of God when God is speaking. This is who the prophet of God is in the bible! As I said in the beginning, the word of God will form and shape the prophet. God's word will always accomplish what it is sent out to do and go where it is sent. God's word never fails! It accomplishes the will of God in the life of the person that has received the word.

The prophet is always in boot camp. God is always renewing the mind of His prophets in boot camp. The reason is to keep the prophets sharp in the word and tuned to the Spirit of God. If you do not know the office how can you be the officer? The true prophet knows who he is in Christ Jesus! God has sent prophets since the beginning of the world by His spoken word, and still is giving prophets to the world today.

Chapter Eleven:
Do You Know the Time?

There are three Greek words that I will use to show the times and seasons that God moves in. The three words are:

1. Chronos: Chronos refers to the general process of time or chronological time.

2. Kairos: Kairos refers to the right time, the opportune or strategic time, the now time.

3. Pleroo: Pleroo refers to the fullness of time.

Chronos is the general time of process or the chronological time. It is being in the hand of God and in process. No prophet moves before the time that God has set. There is a season of process to go through before any other movement may occur. All the prophets in the bible went through the Chronos Time before they could move. Jesus went through the same training, let us look at the scripture where we see Jesus in His Chronos time.

> Matthew 3:16-17. *"And Jesus, when he was baptized, went up straightway out of the water: and, lo, the heavens were opened unto him, and he saw the Spirit of God descending like a dove, and lighting upon him. And lo a voice from heaven, saying, "This is my beloved Son, in whom I am well pleased."*

> Matthew 4: 1. *"Then was Jesus led up of the Spirit into the wilderness to be tempted of the devil."*

The Chronos time starts with Jesus being led into the wilderness at the leading of the Holy Spirit. He did not go on His own. No one gets to choose their Chronos time. God is the one who determines the Chronos time. Reading Luke 4:2-11 we see how Jesus went through His Chronos time in perfect timing guided by the Holy Spirit.

Now we are going to see Chronos move into the Kairos time. Each time has its space to be filled for the purpose to come. One must remember that each time is compartmentalized and must be completed in order to move to the next place.

Kairos is the right time to move, the opportune or strategic time, it is the now time.

> Matthew 4:12-13. *"Now when Jesus had heard that John was cast into prison, he departed into Galilee. And leaving Nazareth, he came and dwelt in Capernaum, which is upon the seacoast, in the borders of Zabulon and Nephthalim:"*

We see that Chronos is moving into Kairos time. We see it in verse 12, Jesus heard that John was in prison, and knew that it was the right time to move into his Kairos time. This is the opportune time that He was waiting, to keep moving in his Kairos time. God moves

John out of the way so Jesus can begin his ministry. We see Chronos and Kairos moving together as one in the opportune time that God had set.

We are now going to see Chronos and Kairos move into Pleroo time. Pleroo is the fullness of time.

> Luke 4:1-2, 14. *"And Jesus being full of the Holy Ghost returned from Jordan, and was led by the Spirit into the wilderness, being forty days tempted of the devil. And in those days he did eat nothing: and when they were ended, he afterward hungered. ...And Jesus returned in the power of the Spirit into Galilee: and there went out a fame of him through all the region round about."*

We now see Pleroo come into its place, the fullness of time. What we see taking place is Jesus being full of the Holy Ghost, then coming in the power of the Spirit. This is the fullness of time. This is the right time for the healing ministry of Jesus. God moves in seasons and He does so strategically. Chronos becomes Kairos, and Kairos becomes Pleroo. Pleroo becomes the fullness of time and the purpose of God. Chronos, Kairos and Pleroo become one.

> 1 Chronicles 12:32. *"And of the children of Issachar, which were men that had understanding of the times, to know what Israel ought to do; the heads of them were two hundred; and all their brethren were at their commandment."*

God trains His Prophets to move in seasons. It is important to know the season that you are in, especially important to what God wants to do in that season that He chooses to move. Moving at the right time with God and not ahead of Him will always make the difference.

1. Chronos refers to the general process of time or to the chronological time.
2. Kairos refers to the right time, the opportune or strategic time, the now time.
3. Pleroo refers to the fullness of time
4. There is a season of process to go through.
5. All the prophets went through Chronos time.
6. Jesus went through the same training.
7. The Chronos time starts with Jesus being led into the wilderness.
8. Chronos is moving into Kairos time.
9. God moves John out of the way.
10. Jesus can begin his ministry.
11. Chronos, Kairos move into Pleroo time.
12. God moves in seasons and He does it strategically.
13. Chronos, Kairos and Pleroo become one.

There is no time better than the timing of God! God moves out of time and into time and is always on time. He is the God of time.

Some words from the book God's Timing for Your Life, by Dutch Sheets.

Appendix:
Descriptions of the Prophets

I. Development of the Prophetic Office

A. The Development of False Prophets

False prophets were in abundance in the heathen nations surrounding God's people. Their medium of revelation was divination and other occult practices [Deuteronomy 18:1-14].

Deuteronomy 13:1-2 and Zechariah 13:2 had its greatest impetus in the time of the monarchy. Apostasy came in the kings of Israel and Judah. True prophets denounced the wicked kings, while these kings viewed the true prophets with suspicion and antagonism. False prophets arose who found it more convenient to be loyal to a corrupt king but disloyal to God. They prophesied for advantage and personal gain [Micah 3:5-11].

B. The Development of True Prophets

Scripture clearly states that the prophetic office has operated from the time of creation: Acts 3:21, *"which God hath spoken by the mouth of all his holy prophets since the world began"*. Luke 11:50-51, *"That the blood of all the prophets which was shed from the foundation of the world, may be required of this generation, From the blood of Abel unto the blood of Zacharias."*

Here Luke indicates that Abel was a prophet. Jeremiah spoke of prophets who were from ancient times [Jeremiah 28:8]. The Gospel writers repeatedly make references to "the prophets of old" [Matthew 5:12, 11:13, 14:5, 16:14, 23:30, Mark 6:15, Luke 1:70, 6:23].

II. The Pre–Mosaic Prophets [4000 – 1450 B.C.]

A. Pre–Patriarchal Prophets. The prophets before Moses, which are identified for us as such are the following:

1. Abel [Luke 11:50 -51].
2. Enoch [Jude 14] who prophesied regarding the second coming of the Lord with ten thousand of his saints.
3. Noah who prophesied concerning the flood and his own descendants [Hebrews 11:7, 1 Peter 3:20, Genesis 9: 25–27].

B. Patriarchal Prophets.

1. Abraham [Genesis 20:7, Psalms 105:9-15].
2. Isaac foretold future events [Psalms 105:9-15, Hebrews 11:20].

3. Jacob [Psalms 105:9-15, Genesis 48:13-49:27] who prophesied over Joseph's son and his own sons.
4. Joseph [Psalms 105:15-23, Genesis 50:24, Hebrews 11:22] who prophesied regarding the future exodus from Egypt.

C. Prophets of the Mosaic Period [1450-1050 B.C.]

1. Moses, who was the first great Hebrew prophet [Deuteronomy 34:10].
2. Miriam, a prophetess [Exodus 15:20].
3. Aaron [Exodus 7:1].
4. Deborah, a prophetess [Judges 4:4].
5. An anonymous prophet [Judges 6:8].
6. Hannah, possibly a prophetess [1 Samuel 2:1-10].

D. Prophets of the Early Monarchy Period [1050-931 B.C.].

The prophetic plea here was mainly national. The prophets spoke of repentance and conversion.

1. Samuel [1 Samuel, Acts 3:24].
2. Nathan [2 Samuel 7:2-17, 12:1-22, 1 Kings 1:8-45].
3. Gad [Samuel 22:5, 1 Chronicles 21:9-19].
4. David [Acts 1:16 2:30, 4:25, Hebrews 11:32].

E. Prophets of the Divided Monarchy Period [931-845 B.C.]

1. Ahijah prophesied the division of the kingdom [1 Kings 11:29].
2. Shemaiah who prophesied to Rehoboam [1 Kings 12:22].
3. Iddo who saw visions against Jeroboam [2 Chronicles 9:26].
4. Jehaziel [2 Chronicles 20:14-24].
5. Eliezer [2 Chronicles 20:37].
6. Two anonymous prophets who prophesied judgment to Jeroboam's house [1 Kings 13].
7. The prophet Jehu who prophesied against Baasha, king of Israel [1 Kings 16:1-7].
8. Hanani, who prophesied a rebuke to Asa, king of Judah [2 Chronicles 16:7].
9. Zechariah, son of Jehoiada the priest, who was slain for his prophetic utterances [Chronicles 24:20-21, Luke 11:50-51].
10. Micaiah who denounced Ahab [1 Kings 22].

11. Elijah prophesied during the time of King Ahab and Jezebel [1 Kings 17–2 Kings 1].
12. Elisha, last of the pre–canonical prophets [2 Kings chapters 2–13].
13. School of the prophets, which overlapped into the time of the canonical prophets [1 Samuel 10 – 5].

F. Prophets of the Canonical Period [845-400 B.C.]

These prophets prophesied of repentance for the divided kingdom. Here they developed the Apocalyptic thrust and the revelation of the future church. Their books contain their prophecies.

1. Pre–exilic Prophets
    a. Obadiah.
    b. Joel.
    c. Jonah.
    d. Amos.
    e. Hosea.
    f. Micah.
    g. Isaiah.
    h. Jeremiah.
    i. Nahum.
    j. Zephaniah.
    k. Habakkuk.
2. Exilic Prophets.
    a. Ezekiel.
    b. Daniel.
3. Post–Exilic Prophets.
    a. Haggai.
    b. Zechariah.
    c. Malachi.

G. Prophets of the Inter-advent Period [400 B.C.–33 A.D.].

1. John the Baptist [Luke 1:76].
2. Zacharias [Luke 1:67].
3. Anna, a prophetess [Luke 2:36].

4. Christ [John 6:14, Luke 4:24, Isaiah 61:1].

H. New Testament Church Prophets [33–100 A.D.].

1. Numerous anonymous prophets of the New Testament church [Acts 11:27].
2. Agabus [Acts 11:27-28].
3. Barnabas [Acts 13:1].
4. Simeon (Niger) [Acts 13:1].
5. Lucius of Cyrene [Acts 13:1].
6. Manaen [Acts 13:1]
7. Judas [Acts 15:32].
8. Silas [Acts 15:32].

It seems evident that at least some of the Apostles were also prophets.

I. Prophets of the Present Age [33 A.D. – Second Coming of Christ]. Prophets continue in this age till Christ's second coming [Ephesians 4:11 – 14, Corinthians 12:28].

III. Description of false Prophets

There are at least thirty references in the old testament to false prophets prophesying. "These" false prophets do not in reality speak for Jehovah but are speaking in their own name things which they themselves have concocted. False prophecy is a presumptuous speaking for God.

A. Old Testament Descriptive Word for False Prophecy. Ziyd. "Presume". A Hebrew word used in the old testament as descriptive of false prophecy is ziyd. Deuteronomy 18:20, "But the prophet, which shall presume (ziyd) to speak a word in my name, which I have not commanded him to speak". The Hebrew word ziyd means "to boil up" or "to seethe". The same Hebrew word is used in the verb form in some passages in the sense of something prepared by cooking [Genesis 25:29]. Thus, the false prophet is "boiling up" something to say. This is in direct contrast with the true prophet whose prophecy simply "bubbles up" [naba]. The false prophecy must be made to "boil up" while the true prophecy "bubbles up". The false prophet "cooks it up" while the true prophet has it "gushing up" [naba] from within him.

B. Classes of false Prophets

1. There were two classes of false prophets in Israel [Deuteronomy 18:20].
    a. "Those false prophets who spake in the name of other gods." These false prophets would advocate going after other gods [Deuteronomy 13:2]. Such

prophets were soundly rejected and deserving of death [Deuteronomy 13:5].

    b. Those false prophets who spoke falsely in Jehovah"s name. The former group was easily discerned by their claim to speak for another god. The latter group, however, was much more difficult to detect as false. Certain tests must be applied to distinguish them from the true prophet.

C. Characteristics of false Prophets

False prophets may be detected by their character and conduct. A false prophet will live a sinful and wicked life, while a true prophet will exemplify conduct and character which are consistent with God's character. A false prophet will bring forth evil fruit, and a true prophet will display good fruit.

> Matthew 7:15-17, *"Beware of false prophets, which come to you in sheep's clothing, but inwardly they are ravening wolves. Ye shall know them by their fruits. Do men gather grapes of thorns, or figs of thistles? Even so every good tree bringeth forth good fruit; but a corrupt tree bringeth forth evil fruit."*

The lives of prophets thus attest to their spiritual authority. False prophets will reveal the following characteristics:

1. Ungodliness in Attitudes.

    False prophets will reveal evil attitudes. These attitudes reflect their perverted nature.

    a. Frivolous and light [Jeremiah 23:32; Zephaniah 3:4].
    b. Treacherous [Zephaniah 3:4].
    c. Opportunistic [Isaiah 30:10-11; Micah 2:11].
    d. Reckless [Isaiah 28:7].
    e. Violent [Matthew 7:15].
    f. Covetous [2 Peter 2:3].
    g. Presumptuous [2 Peter 2:10].
    h. Self-willed [2 Peter 2:10].
    i. Rebellious [2 Peter 2:10].
    j. Despising authority [2 Peter 2:10; Jude 8].
    k. Unwilling to listen to others [1 John 4:6, cf. vs. 1].
    l. Irreverent [Jude 4].
    m. Shameless [Jude 15].
    n. Mocking others [Jude 18].

o. Spirit of superiority [Jude 19].

p. Murmuring and complaining [Jude 26].

2. Ungodliness in Appetites.

False prophets are characterized in scripture as people of low morality. Their desires are perverted.

    a. Profane [Jeremiah 23:11].

    b. Greedy [Micah 3:5, 11].

    c. Immoral [Jeremiah 23:15, 2 Peter 2:2].

    d. Degenerate [Zechariah 13:1-6, Matthew 7:15-20].

    e. Unclean [Peter 2:10].

    f. Lascivious [Jude 4].

    g. Lustful [Jude 18].

3. Ungodliness in Actions.

The evil deeds of the false prophets are the result of their evil hearts. Their works reflect their spiritual depravity. The source of their activity is shown to be unclean or evil spirits [1 Kings 22:19ff, Zechariah 13:1-6].

    a. Prophesied false revelation [Jeremiah 14:14; Ezekiel 22:28].

    b. Drunkards [Isaiah 28:7].

    c. Wickedness [Jeremiah 23:11].

    d. Conspired to deceive [Ezekiel 22:25, 2 Peter 2:3].

    e. Defrauded others [Ezekiel 22:25].

    f. Committed Adultery [Jeremiah 23:14].

    g. Liars [Isaiah 9:15, Jeremiah 23:14, 32].

    h. Supported other Evildoers [Jeremiah 23:14].

    i. Practiced divination [Jeremiah 14:14, Ezekiel 22:28].

    j. Evil speaking [2 Peter 2:12].

    k. False Doctrine [1 John 4:1-2].

4. Figures of False Prophets.

    The following imagery is used:

        a. Dogs

            i. Dumb dogs [Isaiah 56:10].

            ii. Greedy dogs [Isaiah 56:11].

iii. A dog turned to its own vomit [2 Peter 2:22].
- b. Ignorant Shepherds [Isaiah 56:11].
- c. The wind [Jeremiah 5:13].
- d. Slippery ways in the darkness [Jeremiah 23:12].
- e. Chaff [Jeremiah 23:28].
- f. Foxes in the deserts [Ezekiel 13:4].
- g. Lions [Ezekiel 22:25].
    - i. A roaring lion ravening the prey [Ezekiel 22:25].
    - ii. A destroying lion [Jeremiah 2:30].
- h. A fool [Hosea 9:7].
- i. The snare of a fowler [Hosea 9:8].
- j. Ravening wolves [Matthew 7:15].

The parallel passage of 2 Peter chapter 2 and the book of Jude are very graphic in their description of false ministries, especially the false prophet. Both introduce their figurative description with references to Balaam, the classic old testament example of a false prophet [2 Peter 2:15-16; cf. 2:1; Jude 11].

- k. Wells with no water (empty) [2 Peter 2:17].
- l. Clouds carried with a tempest (Promise, but do not produce rain) [2 Peter 2:17].
- m. Mists driven past by a squall of wind (Unstable) [Peter 2:17].
- n. Sunken Rocks (Dangerous) [Jude 12].
- o. Perverted shepherds (Selfish) [Jude 12].
- p. Rainless Clouds (Useless) [Jude 12].
- q. Barren trees (Dead) [Jude 12].
- r. Foaming Sea (Carrying rubbish) [Jude 13].
- s. Wandering stars (Doomed) [Jude 13].

5. Descriptions of True Prophets.
   A. Titles of True Prophets. The titles given to prophets were depict them and their ministry. These titles were descriptive designations, not rising to the rank of formal names. They characterized the true prophet in his prophetic ministry.
   1. Servant of the Lord. This title was descriptive of the prophet's close relation to the Lord in his ministry. He was the Lord's servant. The title stressed the faithfulness and servile character of the prophet's ministry. The term seemed to emphasize that as God's spokesman, the prophet was

doing God's work and fulfilling His purposes in the world. A familiar expression is "My servants the prophet's" [2 Kings 9:7; 17:13; Jeremiah 7:25; Ezekiel 38:17; Zechariah 1:6]. The title was one of high designation.

2. Messenger of the Lord. This title was descriptive of the prophet's relation to the people. They were those sent by God to deliver a message to others. This term was descriptive of the prophet's function. The same Hebrew term was used of angels as God's messengers. The prophets are viewed as "messengers" in Haggai 1:13; 2 Chronicles 36:15-16; Isaiah 44:26; Malachi 3:1.

3. Man of God. This term designated the prophet in relation to his personal character. In contrast to the perverse character of false prophets, the true prophet was God's holy man. It was used of the prophets Moses [Deuteronomy 33:1], Samuel [1 Samuel 9:6], Elijah [1 Kings 17:18, 24], and Elisha [2 Kings 4: 7-9].

4. Man of the Spirit. This title suggested the prophet in relation to his source of revelation. He was a man, moved upon by God's Spirit. This title is found in Hosea 9:7, "the prophet…, the spiritual man [Hebrew-ishharuach, literally, "man of the spirit"]. The term is also descriptive of the New Testament prophet [1 Corinthians 14:37].

5. Anointed One. This term depicted the prophet in relation to his holy calling. He was commissioned and anointed to his office, thus called of God to his prophetic ministry. This title is used of the prophets in 1 Chronicles 16:22 and Psalms 105:15.

6. Seer. This title has been treated in depth. It designated the prophet in relation to his reception of God's revelation. The prophet must "see" before he would speak a prophetic word. Several usages of this term are 1 Samuel 9:9, 2 Samuel 24:11, 1 Chronicles 29:29, 2 Chronicles 29:25 and Amos 7:12.

7. Shepherds [Isaiah 56:11, Ezekiel 34:2-8].This figure designated the prophet in his pastoral occupation as a voice, beckoning a flock of sheep. The prophet was given charge to go to the sheep fold and call to them a message from God.

8. The Stay and the Staff [Isaiah 3:1-2].This figure of the prophets was not exclusive of them but included other leaders of the people [3:2-3]. It described the prophet as a prop which was used of God in his ministry as a support to hold up the people.

9. Bread and Water [Isaiah 3:1-2].This figure was also inclusive of the general leaders of Judah, including the prophet. It depicted the prophet in

his role as a main support of Judah's very existence. He was "bread and water" to Judah and was a feeder of God's word to them.

10. A Watchman [Isaiah 21:6, 11, Ezekiel 3:17, 33:2].This term is most frequently used of all the true prophetic figures. This image likened the prophet to a sentinel on a wall whose duty was to alert the people of the dangers approaching. As faithful watchmen, the prophets warned the people of spiritual peril facing them.

11. A Trumpet Blowing [Isaiah 58:1, Jeremiah 6:17, Ezekiel 33:3-7; 1 Corinthians 14:8].This image described the prophet as sounding an alarm to warn the people. It viewed the prophet's role as a signal to arouse the people to action.

12. Prosecutor in the Heavenly Court [Jeremiah 11:20, Micah 7:9].As God's spokesman, the prophet is pictured as a prosecutor in the court of Heaven, presenting the case before God as judge. As prosecutor of the King's court, he brings to bear before heaven and earth the witness of the Mosaic law against the transgressions of the people. Many of the prophetic messages took on the form of forensic accusations as familiarly used in the prosecutions of the Near Eastern courts.

The familiar Hebrew and Semitic term, riyb is used of the prophets in their prophetic presentations. This Hebrew term regularly was used of a court prosecutor in his listing of legal violations. This Hebrew term riyb is used of the following prophet's declarations: David as prophet [Samuel 24:15, Psalms 43:1], Isaiah [Isaiah 34:8], Jeremiah [Jeremiah 11:20], Ezekiel [Ezekiel 44:24], Hosea [Hosea 4:1, 2:2], and Micah [Micah 6:2, 7:9].

13. A Lion Roaring [Amos 3:7-8].The prophet's voice is likened to a lion's roar, bringing fear to the people so that they may respond to God. Also, the prophet's role as a roaring lion may indicate imminent judgment and destruction.

6. The Prophetess. In Scripture women are not excluded from the prophetic office. There are numerous examples of women called of God to the office as a prophetess [Hebrew, Nebhiah]. In these instances, the prophetess may be speaking or singing prophetically.

  A. The False Prophetess

    1. There were false prophetesses in Ezekiel's time who deceived the people and supported with their prophetic utterances the wicked [Ezekiel 13:17-22].

    2. Noadiah, a prophetess during the restoration period, was aligned with Nehemiah's opposition [Nehemiah 6:14].

3. Jezebel was a false prophetess, pictured in The Book of The Revelation of Jesus Christ. [Revelation 2:20].

B. The True Prophetess
1. Miriam, the sister of Moses, was a prophetess [Exodus 15:20].
2. Deborah, a judge of Israel, was a prophetess [Judges 4:4] who sang prophetic songs [Judges 5:2-31].
3. Hannah, while not called a prophetess, uttered a beautiful prophecy [1 Samuel 2:1-10].
4. Isaiah's wife was called a prophetess [Isaiah 8:2-3].
5. Huldah, was a prophetess, consulted by the high priest at the command of King Josiah [2 Kings 22:14].
6. Anna was a New Testament prophetess [Luke 2:36-38].
7. The four daughters of Philip, the Evangelist, prophesied, although the term "prophetess" is not directly used of them.
8. The Corinthian church expected the regular prophetic ministry of the prophetess [1 Corinthians 11:5].

Women are called today by God to the prophetic office of a prophetess.

From the book by David Blomgren *Prophetic Gatherings In The Church* pages 55 – 64.

The purpose of this manual is for pastors to learn to look for the up and coming young prophets in their ministry. This manual will help them to train them the right way. Not only is this manual for pastors, but also those prophets who have not had the proper training. My prayer is that this manual will get in the hands of seasoned prophets as well as the novice prophets.

www.ingramcontent.com/pod-product-compliance
Lightning Source LLC
LaVergne TN
LVHW061316060426
835507LV00019B/2176